"Cantando" We Learn

Words and Music
by Neraida Smith

National Textbook Company
a division of *NTC Publishing Group* • Lincolnwood, Illinois USA

PREFACE

"Cantando" We Learn (Singing We Learn) is a collection of 20 original songs designed to teach children basic Spanish vocabulary and expressions in a fresh, exciting way. These simple melodies have already delighted many youngsters in their first years of school. The songs are easy *and* fun to sing, making them the ideal medium for introducing the child to the words, accent, and rhythms of the Spanish language.

Through this collection, young people will learn basic greetings in Spanish, numbers, parts of the body, the days of the week, and more. Most of these songs can be looked upon as mini-lessons that open up fundamental areas of the Spanish language to young minds. The simple musical scores contained in this book allow any parent or teacher with a minimal knowledge of, say, the guitar to accompany children as they sing.

A 40-minute cassette tape accompanies this songbook. It features all 20 "Cantando" songs, performed by their composer, Neraida Smith, her children, and several students. These lilting renditions have been expertly recorded and are sure to inspire the young to their best singing efforts. The tape will also provide children with an excellent model for Spanish pronunciation and intonation.

The charming melodies in *"Cantando" We Learn* assure that a child's first introduction to Spanish will be both pleasurable *and* motivating.

1994 Printing

Published by National Textbook Company, a division of NTC Publishing Group.

Manufactured in the United States of America.

3 4 5 6 7 8 9 ML 9 8 7 6 5 4

CONTENTS

¡SÍ, SEÑOR!

Words and Music by
Neraida Smith

¡HOLA!

Words and Music by
Neraida Smith

This is a greeting song. Student 1 (or Group 1) sings and Student 2 (or Group 2) repeats. Sing again, and this time Student 2 (or Group 2) may start the singing.

Hello

Hello! *(echo)* How are you? *(echo)*

Very well. *(echo)* (BOTH PARTS) Thank you. La, la, la,. . . .

DESCANT:

BUENOS DÍAS

Words and Music by
Neraida Smith

Good Morning

Good morning, good morning,
Good morning to you.
Good morning, good morning,
Good morning to you.
Where are you? Here I am, here I am.
Where are you? Here I am, here I am.

The greeting, "good morning," may be substituted by "good afternoon" or "good night" in this song.

Greetings	***Salutaciones***
good morning	*buenos días*
good afternoon	*buenas tardes*
good night	*buenas noches*

¿CÓMO TE LLAMAS?

Words and Music by
Neraida Smith

What's Your Name?

What's your name?
What's your name?
___________ is my name.
What's your name?

The first part of the song should be done as a conversation between two people. What's your name? ___________ is my name.

The rest of the song reinforces colors and demonstrates the suffixes *ito* and *ita*. These diminutive suffixes in Spanish are used to show affection. **Examples:** Blanqu*ito*, Negr*ito*, Roj*ito*.

LOS NÚMEROS

Words and Music by
Neraida Smith

This is a nonsense number song. The song should be done as a finger game.

The Numbers

One, I don't have any.
Two, I have it for you.
Three, you are so fresh!
Four, five,
Six, machete,
Seven, fillet.
Eight, biscuit,
Nine, ten.

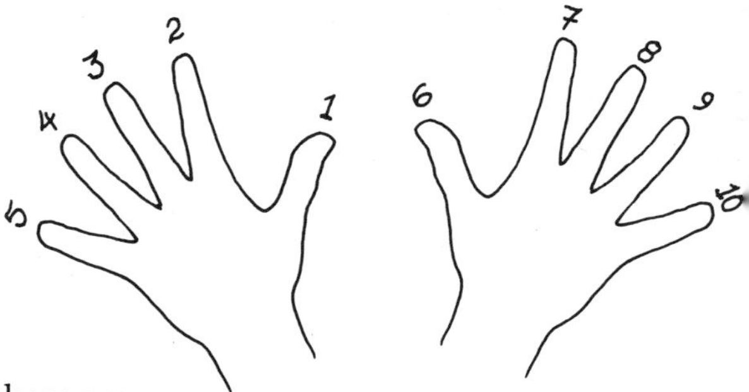

Use resonator bells to play the following measures when the numbers are sung. Assign a different child to each number.

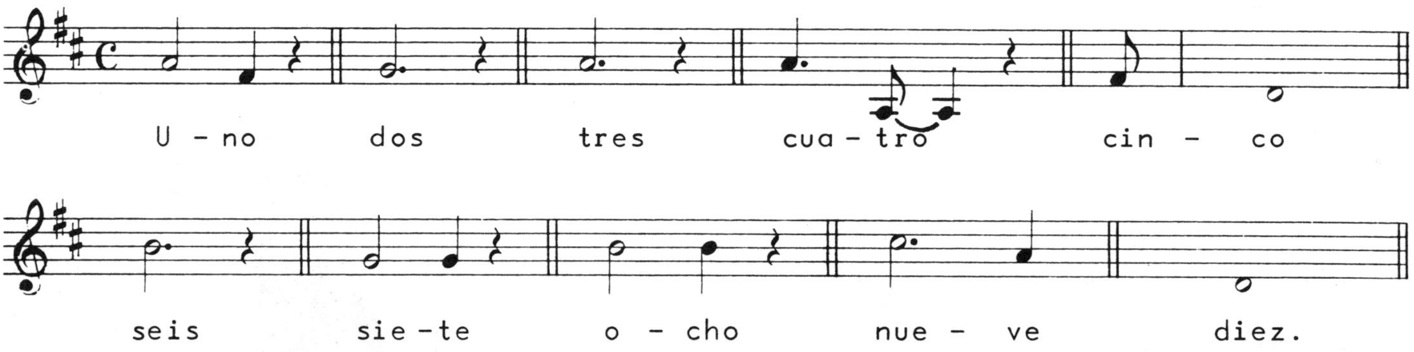

BMI

LOS COLORES

Words and Music by
Neraida Smith

Colors

I've got, I've got,
I've got a hidden color.
Red, green and yellow
White, blue and orange
And the one to guess the color
Will come and put it under.

Children will form a circle. One child will stand in the center of the circle with a small box containing the six colors. The child will hide a color. The child in the center will point to each child in the circle until one guesses the color. The winner comes to the center, puts the color under the box and the game starts again.

LAS VOCALES

Words and Music by
Neraida Smith

The Vowels

The vowels in Spanish.
The vowels in Spanish.
A E I O U
"M" with "a" says "Ma."
"M" with "e" says "Me."
With an "i," it says "Mi."
With an "o," it says "Mo."
"M" with a "u" says "Mu."
Ma Me Mi Mo Mu.

Spanish has only five basic vowel sounds: **A E I O U**

Approximate Sounds in English

A	as in *father*
E	as in *get*
I	as in *machine*
O	as in *owe*
U	as in *boot*

Repeat the song now using other consonant sounds. **Examples:**

L *(ele)*	La	Le	Li	Lo	Lu
F *(efe)*	Fa	Fe	Fi	Fo	Fu
N *(ene)*	Na	Ne	Ni	No	Nu

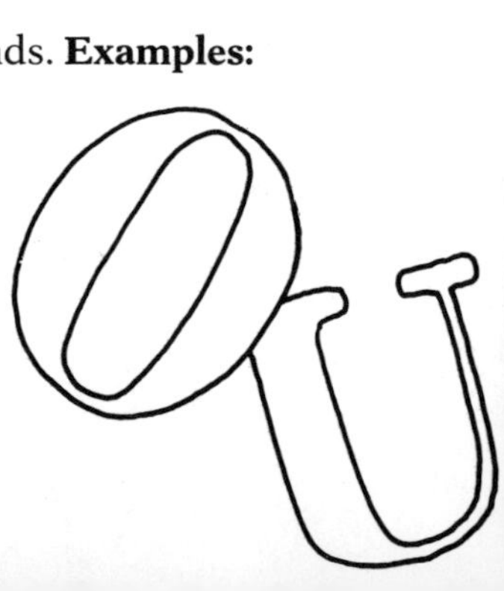

LOS DÍAS DE LA SEMANA

Words and Music by
Neraida Smith

The Days of the Week

Monday and Tuesday. Ay! Ay!
Wednesday, Thursday also.
Friday, Saturday.
One, two, three.
Sunday starts all over again.
Monday, Tuesday, Wednesday,
Thursday, Friday, Saturday, Sunday.

Days	***Días***
Monday	*lunes*
Tuesday	*martes*
Wednesday	*miércoles*
Thursday	*jueves*
Friday	*viernes*
Saturday	*sábado*
Sunday	*domingo*

LOS MESES DEL AÑO

Words and Music by
Neraida Smith

Months of the Year

In the wintertime,
In the wintertime,
December, January and
February.
Springtime,
Springtime,
March, April and
May.
In the summer,
In the summer,
June, July and
August.
Then comes September,
October and November,
Time for autumn.

Months	***Meses***
January	*enero*
February	*febrero*
March	*marzo*
April	*abril*
May	*mayo*
June	*junio*
July	*julio*
August	*agosto*
September	*septiembre*
October	*octubre*
November	*noviembre*
December	*diciembre*

Seasons	***Estaciones***
winter	*invierno*
spring	*primavera*
summer	*verano*
fall	*otoño*

MÚSICA

Words and Music by
Neraida Smith

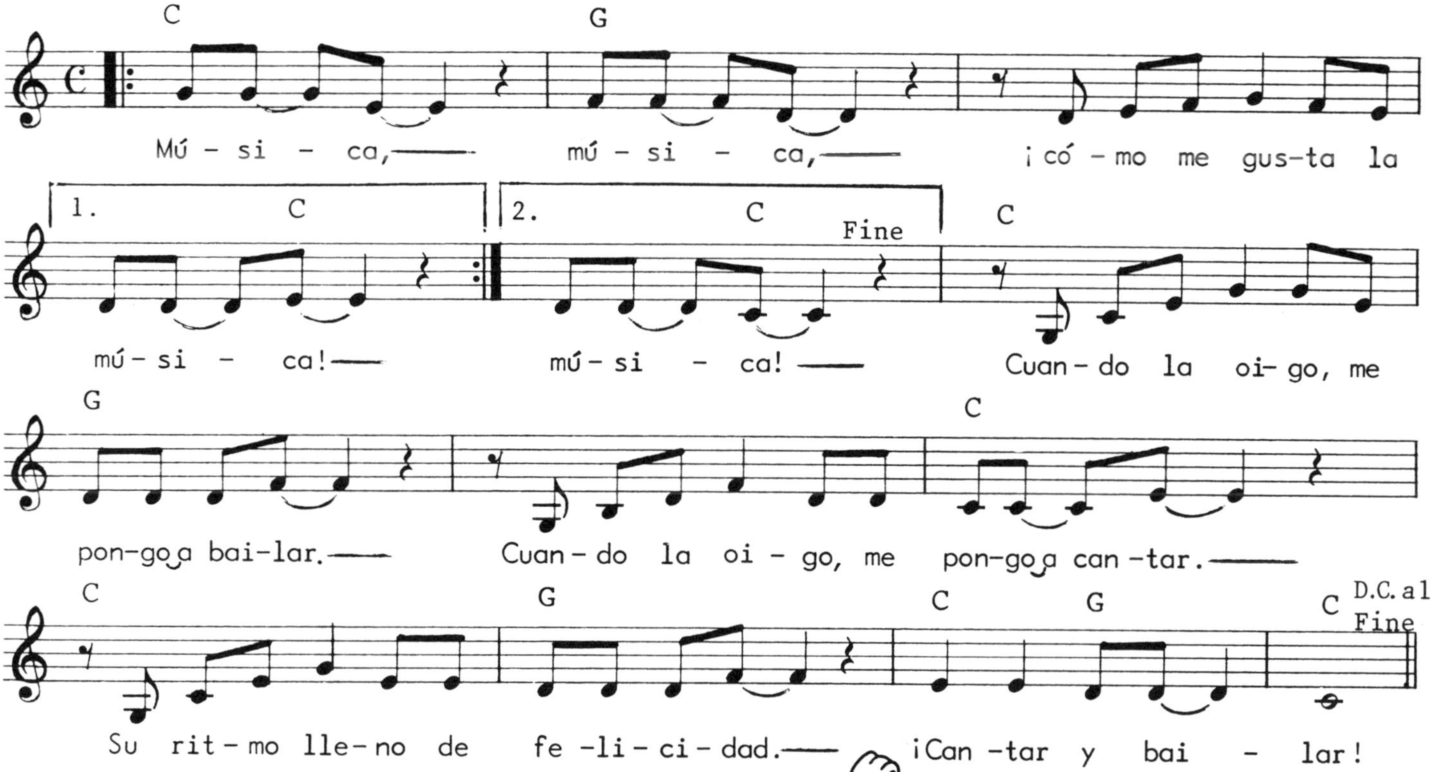

Music
Music, music,
How much I like music!
When I hear music,
I start to dance.
When I hear it,
I start to sing.
Its rhythm fills me
With happiness.
Sing and dance!

Try using rhythm instruments and play along with the song.

CLAVES

BONGOS

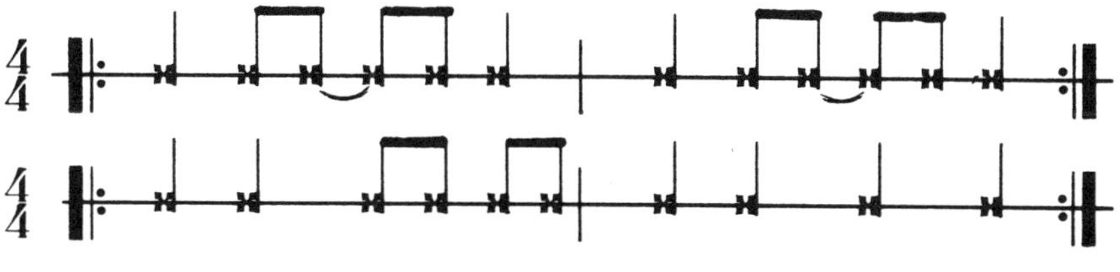

¿CÓMO SE DICE?

Words and Music by
Neraida Smith

How Do You Say It?

How do you say "table"?
How do you say "table"?
How do you say?
How do you say?
How do you say "table"?

For "table" you say "mesa."
For "table" you say "mesa."
For "table" you say,
For "table" you say,
for "table" you say "mesa."

This is a translating game. Different words can be substituted in the song.

Examples:

house	*casa*
chair	*silla*
dog	*perro*
cat	*gato*
boy	*niño*
girl	*niña*

Sí, Sí, Sí

Words and Music by
Neraida Smith

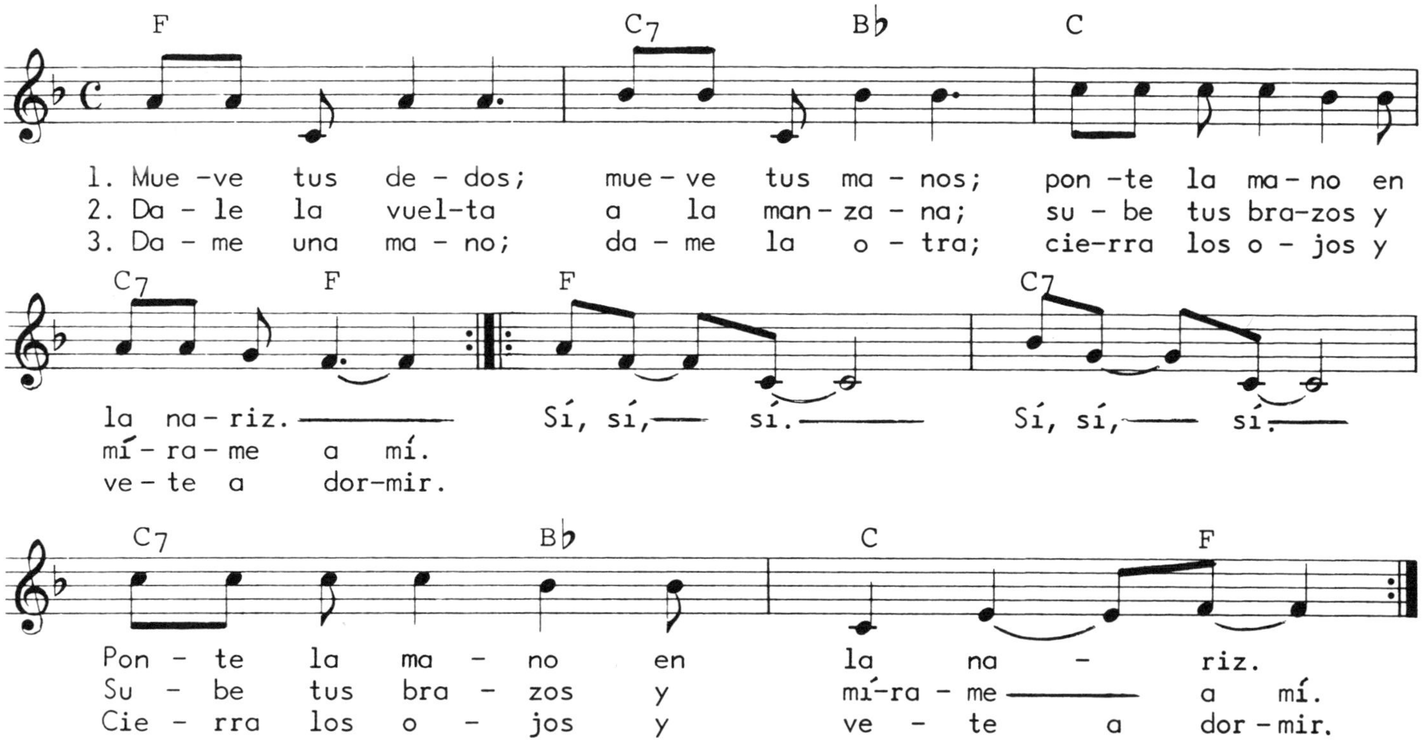

This is an action song. Have the children do motions to the words.

Yes, Yes, Yes

1. Move your fingers,
Move your hands,
Place your hand
On your nose.

Yes, yes, yes.
Yes, yes, yes.
Place your hand
On your nose.

2. Go once
Around the block,
Raise your arms
And look at me.

Yes, yes, yes.
Yes, yes, yes.
Raise your arms
And look at me.

3. Give me one hand,
Give me the other,
Close your eyes
And go to sleep.

Yes, yes, yes.
Yes, yes, yes.
Close your eyes
And go to sleep.

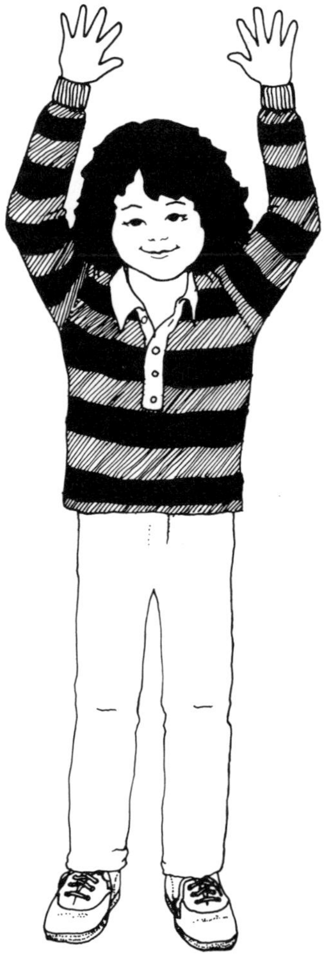

ADIVINA

Words and Music by
Neraida Smith

This song may be used by the children to learn each other's names.

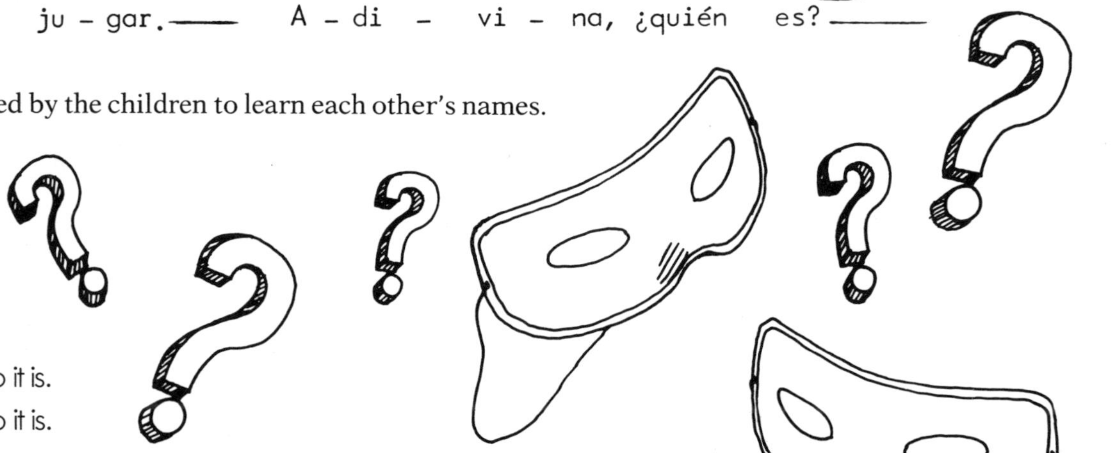

Guess Who?

Guess, guess,
Guess who it is.
Guess, guess,
Guess who it is.
Let's play. Guess who it is.
Let's play. Guess who it is.

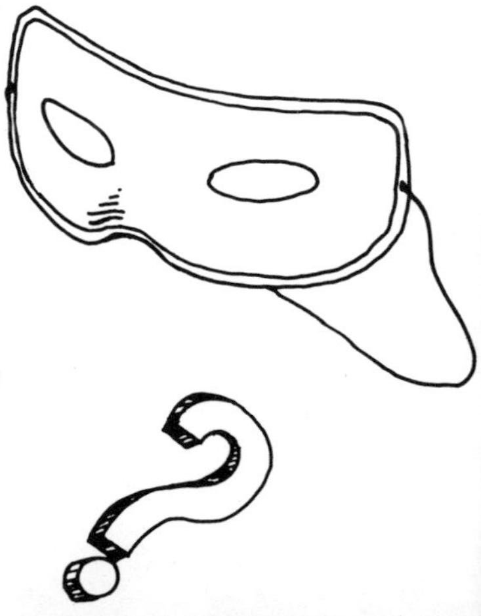

Children walk around in a circle singing the song. One child is in the center of the circle, blindfolded and pointing to the children in the circle. The children stop walking when the song ends, saying, "Adivina, ¿quién es?" (Guess who it is.) The child in the middle tries to guess who it is he (or she) is pointing to. When the guess is correct, the named child goes to the center of the circle and the game starts again.

AL GALLO

Music by
Neraida Smith
Traditional Cuban game

To the Rooster

To the rooster, to the rooster,
The chicken and the horse.
Oh yeah! Oh no!
This is the way to go.

This song can be used as a rhythmic activity.
Example: *(echo clapping)*

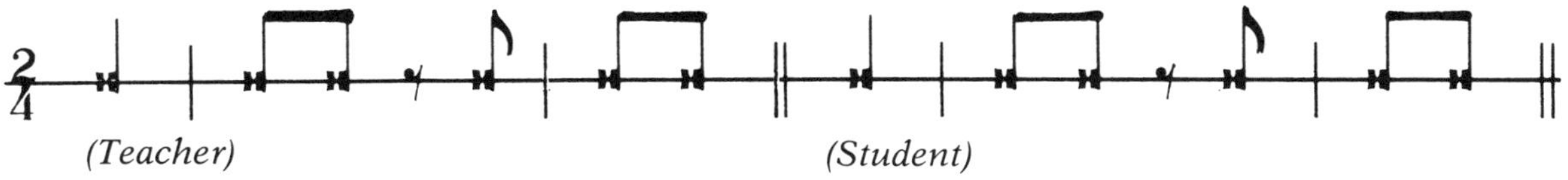

Have fun with the song using finger snaps, stamping the feet or using rhythm sticks. You can also think of other activities of your own. Try a jumping step to the rhythm.

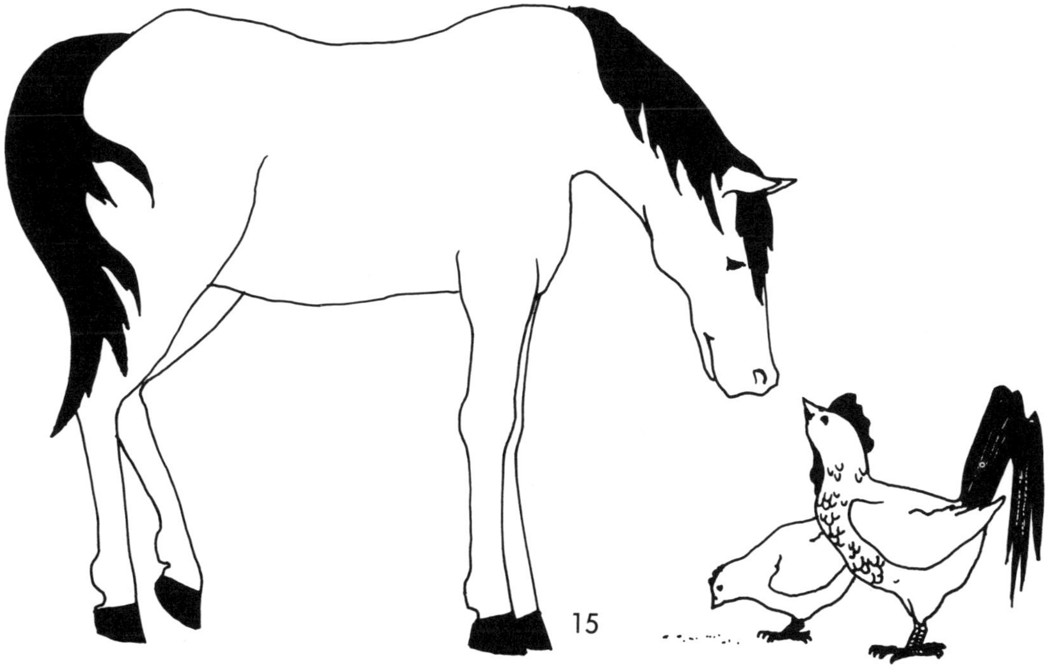

¡ARRIBA! ¡ABAJO!

Words and Music by
Neraida Smith

Do the actions indicated in the song. Tambourines may be used when clapping is indicated.

Up and Down

Two claps up.
Two claps down.
Let's go around.
And let's dance.
Let's go up.
Let's go down.
Good-bye!

CABEZA, CINTURA

Words and Music by
Neraida Smith

Use this song as exercise and to learn the parts of the body. Touch each part of the body as it is mentioned in the song.

Head, Waist, Knees and Feet

Head, waist, knees and feet.
Head, waist, knees and feet.
Head, waist, knees and feet.
Let's sing.

Variation:
Face, eyes,
Nose and mouth. *(3 times)*
Let's sing.

Parts of the Body

head	*cabeza*
waist	*cintura*
knees	*rodillas*
feet	*pies*
face	*cara*
eyes	*ojos*
nose	*nariz*
mouth	*boca*

VAMOS A BAILAR

Words and Music by
Neraida Smith

Let's Dance

This is my friend. *(boy)*	*(Point to a boy.)*
This is my friend. *(girl)*	*(Point to a girl.)*
Let's dance.	*(Dance around.)*
I'm happy to meet you.	*(Shake hands with partner.)*
Good morning.	*(Shake the other hand.)*
I'm happy to meet you.	*(Shake one hand.)*
Good morning.	*(Shake the other hand.)*
Let's dance.	*(Dance around.)*
Good-bye, good-bye.	*(Wave while dancing away.)*
Good-bye, good-bye.	*(Wave while dancing away.)*

Try dancing to this song following the directions above.

A PASEAR

Words and Music by
Neraida Smith

*The children should pantomime motions that are appropriate to putting on the articles of clothing.

I'm Going For a Walk

1. I'm going for a walk.
   I'm going for a walk.
   I put my shirt on,
   And go for a walk.

2. I'm going for a walk.
   I'm going for a walk.
   I put my shirt on,
   My pants,
   And I go for a walk.

3. I'm going for a walk.
   I'm going for a walk.
   I put my shirt,
   My pants and my socks on,
   And I go for a walk.

4. I'm going for a walk.
   I'm going for a walk.
   I put my shirt,
   My pants and my socks on,
   My shoes,
   And I go for a walk.

CHORUS:

For a walk, for a walk.
I'm going for a walk.

LA FIESTA

Words and Music by
Neraida Smith

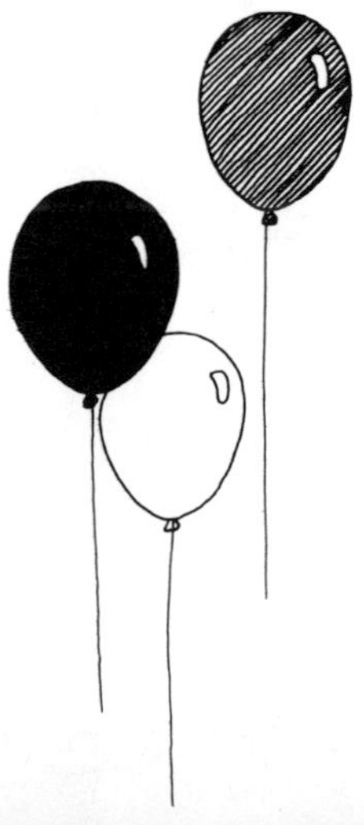

The Party

At the party, at the party,
I'm going to sing.
Let's sing,
At the party, at the party.
The hat, the boots, the suit,
I'm going to sing.

At the party, at the party.
The red, green and white flowers,
At the party, at the party.
Let's sing,
At the party, at the party.

CANTO DE HISPANIDAD

Words and Music by
Neraida Smith

A Song of Friendship

(Hispanic Week song)

A song of friendship.
A song of brothers.
United, we're representing
Our different countries,
Which we dearly love.
It's Hispanic Week.

Whenever you need a hand,
Count on me;
You are my brother.
Let's celebrate
Our happy times.
It's Hispanic Week.

NTC ELEMENTARY SPANISH TEXTS & MATERIALS

Language-Learning Materials
NTC Language Learning Flash Cards
NTC Language Posters
NTC Language Puppets
Welcome to Spanish Learning Cards
Language Visuals
Initial Sounds in Spanish
Ronda del alfabeto (filmstrip/audiocassette)
A, E, I, O, U: Ahora cantas tú
(filmstrip/audiocassette)

Dictionaries
Let's Learn Spanish Picture Dictionary
Spanish Picture Dictionary
Diccionario bilingüe ilustrado

Spanish Language Development Programs
¡Viva el español!
Learning Systems A, B, C
Converso mucho
Ya converso más
¡Nos comunicamos!
Spanish for Young Americans Series
Hablan los niños
Hablan más los niños
Bienvenidos
Welcome to Spanish Series
First Start in Spanish
Moving Ahead in Spanish

Coloring Books
Let's Learn Spanish Coloring Book
My World in Spanish Coloring Book

Workbooks
Mi cuaderno (Books 1, 2, and 3)
Historietas en español
Leamos un cuento
Ya sé leer Workbook

Songbooks
Songs for the Spanish Class
(audiocassette available)
"Cantando" We Learn (audiocassette
available)
Canciones dramatizadas
Christmas Songs in Spanish

Phonics Programs
Soundsalive
Mi primera fonética

Computer Software
Basic Vocabulary Builder on Computer
Amigo: Vocabulary Software

Spanish and Bilingual Readers
Horas encantadas
Mother Goose on the Río Grande
Había una vez
Treasury of Children's Classics
in Spanish and English
¡Hola, amigos! Series
Bilingual Fables
Gabriel, the Happy Ghost Series

For further information or a current catalog, write:
National Textbook Company
a division of *NTC Publishing Group*
4255 West Touhy Avenue
Lincolnwood, Illinois 60646-1975 U.S.A.